EMBRACE THE SUCK

366 DAYS OF STRENGTH, COURAGE, INSPIRATION, WISDOM AND HOPE

GABRIEL A. TOLLIVER

LEGALESE AND CREDITS

BOOK DESIGN: J BIRD LATHON
bopinfomail@gmail.com

PUBLISHED BY BIRDS OF MOTHERSHIP.
creativemothership@gmail.com
TEL: (480) 389-4223

BIRDS OF MOTHERSHIP

DEDICATIONS

This book is dedicated to the
men and women
serving in the Armed Forces and their families and
those
who are no longer with
us.

Mom —
for providing me a spiritual
foundation,
my family and friends who have kept me in their
prayers.

In loving memory
of
William Tolliver Jr.
and
Sandy Summers Head.

Lastly,
my Godson,
Gabriel Paul Bixler —
may you grow up to be a great agent of social
change.

INTRODUCTION

The idea for this book came to me before my first
deployment to Afghanistan for Operation Enduring
Freedom in 2009. The buildup of anxiety, stress and
fear was often overwhelming. The thought of 365+
days in a warzone would be a challenge to my
emotional/spiritual and physical wellbeing. As the
days led up to my unit shipping out, words of
wisdom/inspiration and hope lessened my deployment
anxiety. This book is only a "sample" of
words/thoughts and reflections from a wide spectrum
of individuals who's quotes resonate beyond the
printed/spoken form. I hope these selected quotes
will connect to something inside you - especially
during a life altering experience such as deployment.
It is my hope that these quotes will provide you with
strength, courage, wisdom and faith plus a little bit
of humor and hope to get through each day while
deployed and throughout your life. God Bless.
Peace.

Gabriel A. Tolliver
Kandahar Airfield (KAF)
Afghanistan, 2009-2010

"

All this . . . just a moment in time.

001

The
journey
of a thousand miles
begins
with the first
step.

002

Embrace
The Suck.

IRAQ WAR
SLANG

Have I not
commanded
you to be strong and
courageous?
Do not be
afraid,
do not be
discouraged
for the Lord God
will
be with you wherever you
go.

**JOSHUA
1:9**

004

No matter how
far
a person can
go,
the horizon is
still
way beyond
you.

**ZORA NEALE
HURSTON**

00

Prepare for the
unknown
by studying how
others
in the past have
coped
with the
unforeseeable
and the
unpredictable.

**GEORGE S.
PATTON**

006

Never doubt that a small
group
of thoughtful committed
citizens
can change the
world.
Indeed, it is the
only
thing that ever
has.

**MARGARET
MEAD**

007

War
is the ultimate
reality
based horror
show.

**DAVID
HACKWORTH**

008

Power in defense of
freedom
is greater than
power
in behalf of
tyranny
and
oppression.

**EL-HAJJ MALIK
EL-SHABAZZ**

009

Do not dwell in the
past,
do not dream of the
future,
concentrate the
mind
on the present
moment.

BUDDHA

010

I eat a
slice
of humble pie
everyday.

**MSG MUNOZ-DONES
KAF**

011

You can often measure a
person
by the size of his
dream.

ROBERT H. SCHULLER

012

Fill up the crevices of
time
with the things that matter
most.

**AMY
CARMICHAEL**

013

The beginning is the
most
part of the
work.

PLATO

14

There is no such
thing
as a insignificant
enemy.

**SPANISH
PROVERB**

015

Make no little
plans;
they have no
magic
to stir blood and probably
themselves
will not be realized. Make big
plans;
Aim high in hope and
work.

**DANIEL H.
BURNHAM**

016

Think of the
world
you carry within
you.

**RAINER MARIA
RILKE**

017

I would rather
walk
with God in the
dark
than go alone in the
light.

MARY GARDI
BRAIN

18

Every person you meet
knows
something you don't.
Learn
from them.

H. JACKSON BROWN

019

A gentle
word,
a kind
look
a good natured
smile
can work
wonders
and accomplish
miracles.

**WILLIAM
HAZLITT**

020

It takes
guts
to get out of the
ruts.

**ROBERT H.
SCHULLER**

021

I have not
yet
begun to
fight!

**JOHN PAUL
JONES**

022

Excellence
is not a
skill.
It is an
attitude.

**RALPH
MARSTEN**

023

War
is not meant to be you
dying
for your
country-
it is by
making
the other
bastard
die for
his.

**GEORGE S.
PATTON**

024

A man's
country
is not a certain area of
land,
of mountains, rivers, and
woods,
but it is a principle and
patriotism
is loyalty to that
principle.

**GEORGE WILLIAM
CURTIS**

025

When angry, count to four; when very angry, swear.

MARK TWAIN

026

The first
casualty
when war comes is
truth.

**HIRAM
JOHNSON**

027

Sweat saves
blood,
blood saves
lives,
and brains saves
both.

**ERWIN
ROMMEL**

028

I believe that every
person
is born with
talent.

MAYA
ANGELOU

029

Patriots always talk of
dying
for their
country
and never of
killing
for their
country.

**BERTRAND
RUSSELL**

030

Older men declare
war.
But it is the
youth
that must fight and
die.

**HERBERT
HOOVER**

031

It is well that

war

is so terrible. *Otherwise,* We should

grow

too fond of

it.

**ROBERT E.
LEE**

032

An unjust
peace
is better than a just
war.

**MARCUS TULLIUS
CICERO**

033

Winning
starts with
beginning.

**ROBERT H.
SCHULLER**

034

All
war
is
deception.

SUN
TZU

035

A soldier will
fight
long and hard for a
bit
of colored
ribbon.

**NAPOLEON
BONAPARTE**

036

I accept
reality
and dare not
question
it.

**WALT
WHITMAN**

037

It isn't enough to
talk
about peace. One must
believe
in it. And it isn't
enough
to believe in it.
One
must work at
it.

**ELEANOR
ROOSEVELT**

038

Nobody
can bring
you
peace but
yourself.

**RALPH WALDO
EMERSON**

039

There's a world of
difference
between truth and facts.
Facts
can obscure the
truth.

MAYA
ANGELOU

040

Live
as if you were to
die
tomorrow,
learn
as if you were to live
forever.

**MAHATMA
GANDHI**

041

Ten soldiers wisely
led
will beat a hundred without a
head.

EURIPEDES

042

There are no
failures,
just experiences and your
reaction
to them.

**TOM
KRAUSE**

043

Trust only
movement.
Life happens at the level of
events,
not of words.   Trust
movement.

**ALFRED
ADLER**

044

No man
make
another
free.

**ZORA NEALE
HURSTON**

045

A person is a
person
because he
recongnizes
others as
persons.

**BISHOP DESMOND
TUTU**

046

Never underestimate your
problem
or your ability to
deal
with it.

**ROBERT H.
SCHULLER**

047

Don't compromise
yourself.
You are all
you
got.

**JANIS
JOPLIN**

048

Great works are
performed
not by strength but by
perserverance.

049

Look at life through the
windshield,
not the rearview
mirror.

**BYRD
BAGGETT**

050

Life
loves
the
liver
of
it.

**MAYA
ANGELOU**

051

People learn to
lead
because they
care
about something.

**CHARLOTTE
BUNCH**

052

They can
conquer
who believe they
can.

**RALPH WALDO
EMERSON**

053

You will encounter many
distractions
and many
temptations
to put your goal
aside:
The security of a job,
a wife
who wants kids,
whatever.
But if you hang in there,
always
following your
vision,
I have no
doubt you will
succeed.

**LARRY
FLINT**

054

It's easier to
resist
at the
beginning
than at the
end.

**LEONARDO
DA VINCI**

055

Even death
is
not to be
feared
by one
who
has lived
wisely.

BUDDHA

056

Life itself is always a
trial.
In training, you must
test
and polish yourself in order to
face
the great challenges of
life.
Trascend the realm of life and
death,
and then you will be able to
make
your way calmly and safely
through
any crises that confronts
you.

**MORIHEI
UESHIBA**

057

War
does not
determine
who is
right
only who is
left.

BERTRAND RUSSELL

058

All that is
essential
for the triumph of
evil
is that
good
men do
nothing.

**EDMUND
BURKE**

059

Press on.
Obstacles
are seldom the same size
tomorrow
as they are
today.

ROBERT H. SCHULLER

060

Live your
life
that the fear of
death
can never enter your
heart.

TECUMSEH

061

While I know
myself
as a
creation
of God, I am also
obligated
to realize and
remember
that everyone else and
everything
else are also God's
creation.

**MAYA
ANGELOU**

062

A real
friend
is one who walks
in
when the
rest
of the world walks
out.

**WALTER
WINCHELL**

063

The mind is
everything,
What you think you
become.

BUDDHA

064

The real
voyage
of discovery
consists
not in seeking new
landscapes,
but in having new
eyes.

**MARCEL
PROUST**

065

Better to fight for
something
than live for
nothing.

**GEORGE S.
PATTON**

066

If you don't stand for
something
you will fall for
anything.

**EL-HAJJ MALIK
EL-SHABAZZ**

067

Wars may be fought with
weapons,
but they are won by
men.
It is the
spirit
of men who
follow
and of the man who
leads
that gains the
victory.

**GEORGE S.
PATTON**

068

Society has always seemed to demand
a little more from human beings
than it will get in practice.

**GEORGE
ORWELL**

069

Do not go where the path may
lead.
Go instead where there is no
path
and leave a
trail.

**RALPH WALDO
EMERSON**

070

Truth
is on the
side
of the
oppressed.

**EL-HAJJ MALIK
EL-SHABAZZ**

071

Peace is not something you
wish
for: It's something you
make,
something you
do,
something you
are
and something you
give
away.

**ROBERT
FULGHUM**

072

Some people are at the
top
of the ladder, some are in the
middle,
still more are at the
bottom,
and a whole lot
more
don't even
know
there is a
ladder.

**ROBERT H.
SCHULLER**

073

I have
found
that among its other
benefits,
giving liberates the
soul
of the
giver.

**MAYA
ANGELOU**

074

No matter how
far
you have
gone
on the wrong
road,
turn
back.

**TURKISH
PROVERB**

075

Vision without
actions
is a
daydream,
action without
vision
is a
nightmare.

**JAPANESE
PROVERB**

076

Faith is to
believe
what we don't
see;
and the
reward
of this
faith
is to
see
what we
believe.

AUGUSTINE

077

Change is
inevitable
except from a vending
machine.

ROBERT C.
GALLAGHER

078

Show respect to all
people,
but grovel to
none.

TECUMSEH

079

He
who
angers
you
conquers
you.

ELIZABETH KENNY

080

Get
mad, then
get
over
it.

081

Nothing lasts
forever
it's just a moment in
time.

**CHRISTOPHER LEE
TOLLIVER**

082

A sense of
humor
is a major
defense
against minor
troubles.

**MIGNON
MCLAUGHLIN**

083

Nothing
will
work
unless
you
do.

**MAYA
ANGELOU**

084

Be
curious,
not
judgmental.

**WALT
WHITMAN**

085

Spectacular
achievement
is
always
preceded
by
unspectacular
preparation.

**ROBERT H.
SCHULLER**

086

Every
moment
of
light
and
dark
is a
miracle.

**WALT
WHITMAN**

087

I have never advocated
war
except as a means of
peace.

**ULYSSES S.
GRANT**

088

If it's natural to
kill,
how come
men
have to go into
training
to learn
how?

JOAN
BAEZ

089

In peace,
sons
bury their
fathers.
In war,
fathers
bury their
sons.

HERODOTUS

090

Never think that
war,
no matter how
necessary,
nor how
justified,
is not a
crime.

**ERNEST
HEMINGWAY**

091

All men are
prepared
to accomplish the
incredible
if their ideals are
threatened.

**MAYA
ANGELOU**

092

Sometime
they'll give a
war
and nobody will
come.

**CARL
SANDBURG**

093

Bitterness is like
cancer.
It eats upon the
host.
But anger is like
fire.
It burns it all
clean.

**MAYA
ANGELOU**

094

The
friend
of a
friend
is my
friend.

**AFRICAN
PROVERB**

095

The
enemy
of my
enemy
is my
friend.

**ARAB
PROVERB**

096

War
grows out of the
desire
of the
individual
to gain
advantage
at the
expense
of his fellow
man.

**NAPOLEON
HILL**

097

Today's
accomplishments
were yesterday's
impossibilities.

**ROBERT H.
SCHULLER**

098

War is a series of
catastrophes
which result in
victory.

ALBERT
PIKE

099

Battle
is
an
orgy
of
disorder.

**GEORGE S.
PATTON**

100

War
is
hell.

**WILLIAM TECUMSEH
SHERMAN**

101

War
is only a cowardly
escape
from the
problems
of
peace.

**THOMAS
MANN**

102

It seems like such a terrible
shame
that innocent
civilians
have to get hurt in
wars,
otherwise combat would
be
such a wonderfully
healthy
way to rid the human
race
of unneeded
trash.

**FRED
WOODWORTH**

103

I
must study politics and
war
that my
sons
may have
liberty
to study
mathematics
and
philosophy.

**JOHN
ADAMS**

104

Achievement
brings its own
anticlimax.

**MAYA
ANGELOU**

105

Have you
heard
that it was
good
to gain the day? I also
say
it is good to
fall,
battles are
lost
in the same
spirit
in which they are
won.

**WALT
WHITMAN**

106

The important
thing
is not to stop
questioning.

**ALBERT
EINSTEIN**

107

You can turn
painful
situations around through
laughter.
If you can find
humor
in anything, even
poverty,
you can
survive
it.

BILL COSBY

108

Every
gun
that is made, every
warship
launched, every
rocket
fired, signifies in the
final
sense a theft from those who
hunger
and are not
fed,
those who are
cold
and are not
clothed.

**DWIGHT D.
EISENHOWER**

109

A visitor from Mars
could easily pick out the civilized
nations. They have the best
implements of war.

HERBERT V. PROCHNOW

110

Have you learned the
lessons
only of those who admired
you,
and were tender with
you,
and stood aside for
you?
Have you not learned great
lessons
from those who braced
themselves
against you,
and disputed passage with
you?

**WALT
WHITMAN**

111

Fear thou not; for
I
am with thee:
be
not dismayed; for I am thy God:
I
will strengthen thee; yea,
I
will help thee; yea,
I
will uphold thee with the
right
hand of my
righteousness.

**ISAIAH
41:10**

112

Everyone's a
pacifist
between wars. It's like being a
vegetarian
between meals.

**COLMAN
MCCARTHY**

113

All wars are
civil
wars, because all men are
brothers.

**FRANCOIS
FENELON**

114

All changes, even the most
longed
for, have their
melancholy;
for what we leave
behind
us is a part of
ourselves;
we must die to
one
life before we can enter
another.

**ANATOLE
FRANCE**

115

Courage
is the most
important
of all the
virtues,
because without
courage
you can't
practice
any other
virtue
consistently. You can
practice
any virtue erratically, but
nothing
consistently without
courage.

**MAYA
ANGELOU**

116

All change is not
growth,
as all movement is not
forward.

**ELLEN
GLASGOW**

117

Always remember that the future comes one day at a time.

DEAN ACHESON

118

Because things
are
the way they
are,
things will not
stay
the way they
are.

**BERTOLT
BRECHT**

119

Keep it movin'.

**DOUGLAS
TOLLIVER**

120

We must use time
creatively.

**MARTIN LUTHER
KING, JR.**

121

Change
alone is eternal, perpetual,
immortal.

**ARTHUR
SCHOPENHAUER**

122

He that will not apply new
remedies
must expect new
evils;
for time is the greatest
innovator.

**FRANCIS
BACON**

123

It is
difficult
to say what is
impossible,
for the dream of
yesterday
is the hope of
today
and the reality of
tomorrow.

**ROBERT H.
SCHULLER**

124

Ignorance is no
excuse,
it's the real
thing.

**IRENE
PETER**

125

Most of the
change
we think we see in
life
is due to
truths
being in and out of
favor.

**ROBERT
FROST**

126

Love recognizes no
barriers.
It jumps hurdles, leaps fences,
penetrates
walls to arrive at it
destination
full of
hope.

**MAYA
ANGELOU**

127

It's the most
unhappy
people who most
fear
change.

**MIGNON
MCLAUGHLIN**

128

Only the wisest and
stupidest
of men never
change.

CONFUCIOUS

129

Things
do not change;
we
change.

**HENRY DAVID
THOREAU**

130

When you jump for
joy,
beware that no
one
moves the
ground
from beneath your
feet.

**STANISLAW
JERZY LEC**

131

Whoever is
happy
will make
others
happy too.

**ANNE
FRANK**

132

Keep your
face
always toward the
sunshine
and shadows
will
fall behind
you.

133

Stop.
Look.
Listen.
Think about it.

ANONYMOUS

134

We sleep
safe
in our beds because rough
men
stand ready in the
night
to visit
violence
on those
who
would do us
harm.

**GEORGE
ORWELL**

135

What can you
do
except deal with
it?

TOM
RODDHA

136

What great
thing
would you
attempt
if you knew
you
could not
fail?

**ROBERT H.
SCHULLER**

137

How important it is for
us
to recognize and
celebrate
our heroes and
sheroes.

**MAYA
ANGELOU**

138

Do you know the
difference
between education and
experience?
Education is when
you
read the fine print;
experience
is what you get
when you
don't.

**PETE
SEEGER**

139

Experience is one
thing
you can't get for
nothing.

140

Everything has been said
before,
but since nobody
listens
we have to keep
going
back and
beginning
all over
again.

**ANDRE
GIDE**

141

Good judgment comes from experience, and often experience comes from bad judgment.

RITA MAE BROWN

142

Life is the
art
of drawing without an
eraser.

**JOHN W.
GARDNER**

143

Life can only be understood
backwards,
but it must be lived
forward.

**SOREN
KIERKEGAARD**

144

For every
minute
you remain
angry,
you give up sixty
seconds
of peace of
mind.

**RALPH WALDO
EMERSON**

145

The best
weapon
against an
enemy
is another
enemy.

**FRIEDRICH
NIETZCHE**

146

When anger rises,
think
of the
consequences.

CONFUCIOUS

147

How can a
society
that exists on
instant
mashed potatoes, packaged cake
mixes,
frozen dinners, and
instant
cameras teach
patience
to its
young?

**PAUL
SWEENEY**

148

If you don't like
something,
change it. If
you
can't change
it,
change your
attitude.

**MAYA
ANGELOU**

149

Tough times never
last,
but tough people
do.

**ROBERT H.
SCHULLER**

150

I've failed
over
and over
again
in my
life
and that
is
why I
succeed.

MICHAEL JORDAN

151

It is
not
if you fall
down,
rather if you get back
up
that defines your
courage.

SANTIAGO

152

Have the
courage
to say
no.
Have the
courage
to face the
truth.
Do the
right
thing because it is
right.
These are the magic
keys
to living your life with
integrity.

**W. CLEMENT
STONE**

153

All that is to
break
the spell of
inertia
and frustrations is this:
Act
as if it were impossible to
fail.

**DOROTHEA
BRANDE**

154

Experience is the best teacher.

FRANCES M. WHITCHER

155

Those who don't got
it,
can't show
it.
Those who got
it,
can't hide
it.

**ZORA NEALE
HURSTON**

156

Do your
damnedest
in an
ostentatious
manner all the
time.

**GEORGE S.
PATTON**

157

There is no better than
adversity.
Every defeat, every
heartbreak,
every loss,
contains
its own
seed,
its own
lesson
on how to
improve
your performance the next
time.

**EL-HAJJ MALIK
EL-SHABAZZ**

158

Progress is the
attraction
that moves
humanity.

**MARCUS
GARVEY**

159

Life loves to be
taken
by the
lapel
and told:
"I'm
with you kid. Let's
go."

MAYA
ANGELOU

160

There is no easy
path
leading out of
life
and few easy
ones
that lie within
it.

**WALTER SAVAGE
LANDOR**

161

Knowledge in youth, wisdom in age.

PROVERB

162

When you can't
solve
the problem, manage
it.

**ROBERT H.
SCHULLER**

163

It is difficult to inspire
others
to accomplish what
you
haven't been willing to
try.

ANONYMOUS

164

If your actions
inspire
others to
dream
more, learn more,
do
more and become more,
you
are a
leader.

**JOHN QUINCY
ADAMS**

165

Don't tell people
how
to do things, tell them
what
to do and let them
surprise
you with their
results.

**GEORGE S.
PATTON**

166

Humor
is mankind's greatest
blessing.

167

All things appear and
disappear
because of the
concurrence
of causes and
conditions.
Nothing ever exists entirely
alone;
everything is in
relation
to everything
else.

BUDDHA

168

The secret to
happiness
is not doing what one
likes
but in
liking
what one has to
do.

**J.M.
BARRIE**

169

Be content with your
surrounding
but not with
yourself
till you have
made
the most of
them.

ANONYMOUS

170

We may encounter many
defeats
but we
must
not be
defeated.

**MAYA
ANGELOU**

171

Time goes by fast,
people
go in and out of your
life.
You must never miss the
opportunity
to tell these
people
how much
they
mean to
you.

ANONYMOUS

172

People come into your
life
and people leave your
life.
You have to trust that
life
has a road
mapped
out for
you.

**ORLANDO
BLOOM**

173

Life is too
short
to be
living
somebody else's
dreams.

**HUGH
HEFNER**

174

I don't
measure
a man's
success
by how high he
climbs
but how high he
bounces
when he hits
bottom.

**GEORGE S.
PATTON**

175

Let your
hopes,
not your
hurts,
shape your
future.

**ROBERT H.
SCHULLER**

176

If you
smell
yourself too much,
you
might be
stinkin'.

LIL' BLACK GABE

177

Have compassion for all
beings,
rich and poor alike;
each
has their
suffering.
Some suffer too
much,
others too
little.

BUDDHA

178

It is unwise to be too
sure
of one's own
wisdom.
It is healthy to be
reminded
that the strongest might
weaken
and the wisest might
err.

**MAHATMA
GANDHI**

179

God asks no
one
whether he will
accept
life. That
is
not the choice.
You
must take
it.
The choice is
how.

**HENRY WARD
BEECHER**

180

A great
dream
begins with a
dreamer.
Always remember, you have
within
you the strength, the
patience,
and the
passion
to reach for the
stars
to change the
world.

HARRIET TUBMAN

181

There is nothing so
pitiful
as a young
cynic
because he has
gone
from knowing
nothing
to believing
nothing.

**MAYA
ANGELOU**

182

There are years that ask questions
and there are years that answer.

ZORA NEALE HURSTON

183

Faith is
taking
the first
step
even when you don't
see
the whole
staircase.

**MARTIN LUTHER
KING, JR.**

184

Few people even
scratch
the surface, much less
exhaust
the contemplation of their own
experience.

**RANDOPLH
BOURNE**

185

The years
teach
much which the days never
know.

**RALPH WALDO
EMERSON**

186

In these
times
you have to be an
optimist
to open your
eyes
when you
awake
in the
morning.

**CARL
SANDBURG**

187

There is
nothing
so easy to
learn
as experience and
nothing
so hard to
apply.

**JOSH
BILLINGS**

188

Wait. Be
patient.
The storm will
pass.
The spring will
come.

**ROBERT H.
SCHULLER**

189

Action and
reaction,
ebb and flow,
trial and error,
change -
this is the rhythm of
living.
Out of our over-confidence,
fear;
out of our
fear,
clearer vision, fresh
hope.
And out of hope,
progress.

**BRUCE
BARTON**

190

Courage is
fear
holding on a minute
longer.

**GEORGE S.
PATTON**

191

If you're
not
ready to
die
for it, put the word
'freedom'
out of your
vocabulary.

**EL-HAJJ MALIK
EL-SHABAZZ**

192

There is a very fine
line
between loving
life
and being greedy for
it.

193

A dog is not considered a good
dog
because he is a good
barker.
A man is not considered a good
man
because he is a good
talker.

BUDDHA

194

It's better to conceal one's
knowledge
than to display one's
ignorance.

**SPANISH
PROVERB**

195

Weakness of attitude,
becomes
weakness of
character.

**ALBERT
EINSTEIN**

196

True silence is the
rest
of the
mind;
It is to the
spirit
what sleep is to the
body,
nourishment and
refreshment.

**WILLIAM
PENN**

197

Knowledge is
proud
that it
knows
so much;
wisdom
is humble that it knows no
more.

198

He is able who
thinks
he is
able.

BUDDHA

199

Who dares
wins.

**BRITISH ARMY S.A.S.
(SPECIAL AIR SERVICE)
MOTTO**

200

If there is no
struggle,
there is no
progress.

**FREDERICK
DOUGLASS**

201

Most people who
succeed
in the face of seemingly
impossible
conditions are
people
who simply
don't
know how to
quit.

**ROBERT H.
SCHULLER**

202

Freedom --
to walk
free
and own no
superior.

203

It is time for
parents
to teach young
people
early on that in
diversity
there is
beauty
and there is
strength.

**MAYA
ANGELOU**

204

No country can act
wisely
simultaneously in every
part
of the
globe
at every moment of
time.

**HENRY A.
KISSINGER**

205

Ours is a
world
of nuclear
giants
and ethical
infants.
We know more about
war
that we know about
peace,
more about
killing
that we know about
living.

**OMAR N.
BRADLEY**

206

War
is not an
adventure.
It is a
disease.
It is like
typhus.

**ANTOINE
DE SAINT EXUPERY**

207

The basic
problems
facing the
world
today are not
susceptible
to a military
solution.

**JOHN F.
KENNEDY**

208

Believers, look
up -
take courage. The
angels
are nearer than you
think.

**BILLY
GRAHAM**

209

Come close to
God,
and God
will
come close to
you.

**JAMES
4:8**

210

So I tell
you,
whatever you
ask
for in
prayer,
believe that you have
received
it, and it will be
yours.

**MARK
11:24**

211

Prayer
is simply a two way
conversation
between you and
God.

BILLY GRAHAM

212

There are no
U-Hauls
on the back of
hearses.

**BESSIE H.
TOLLIVER**

213

No one can excel in
everything.
The decades
demand
decisions. Choose
wisely.
Your choices
pinpoint
your priorities and
determine
your destiny. Use
it
or lose
it.

ANONYMOUS

214

What appears to be the
end
of the
road
may simply be a
bend
in the
road.

**ROBERT H.
SCHULLER**

215

An idea that is
developed
and put into
action
is more
important
than an
idea
that exists
only
as an
idea.

BUDDHA

216

What one has not
experienced,
one will
never
understand in
print.

217

If we lose
love
and self
respect
for each
other,
this is
how
we finally
die.

**MAYA
ANGELOU**

218

Untutored courage is
useless
in the
face
of educated
bullets.

**GEORGE S.
PATTON**

219

Without education,
you
are not going
anywhere
in this
world.

**EL-HAJJ MALIK
EL-SHABAZZ**

220

He who experiences the
unity
of life
sees
his own
Self
in all
beings,
and all
beings
in his own
Self,
and looks on
everything
with an impartial
eye.

BUDDHA

221

Experience is the mother of truth; and by experience we learn wisdom.

WILLIAM SHIPPEN, JR.

222

The only
source
of knowledge is
experience.

**ALBERT
EINSTEIN**

223

Stumbling
is not
falling.

**EL-HAJJ MALIK
EL-SHABAZZ**

224

Watch
what people are
cynical
about, and
one
can often
discover
what they
lack.

**GEORGE S.
PATTON**

225

If one is
lucky,
a solitary
fantasy
can totally
transform
one million
realities.

**MAYA
ANGELOU**

226

When the legends
die,
the dreams end;
there
is no more
greatness.

TECUMSEH

227

Never bring the
problem
solving stage into the
decision
making stage. Otherwise, you
surrender
yourself to the
problem
rather than the
solution.

**ROBERT H.
SCHULLER**

228

Experience
is simply the
name
we give our
mistakes.

229

Experience is the child of
thought,
and thought is the child of
action.

**BENJAMIN
DISRAELI**

230

Experience
keeps a dear
school,
but fools will
learn
in no
other.

**BENJAMIN
FRANKLIN**

231

Don't turn
your
back on
wisdom,
for she will protect you.
Love
her and she will guard
you.
Getting wisdom is the
wisest
thing you can
do.
And whatever else you
do,
develop good
judgement.

**PROVERBS
4:6 - 7**

232

Every human
being
is the
author
of his
own
health or
disease.

BUDDHA

233

In all our
deeds,
the proper
value
and respect for time
determines
success or
failure.

**EL-HAJJ MALIK
EL-SHABAZZ**

234

The time to take counsel of your
fears
is before you make an important
battle
decision. That's the time to
listen
to every fear you can
imagine!
When you have collected all the
facts
and fears and made your
decision,
turn off all your
fears
and go
ahead!

**GEORGE S.
PATTON**

235

Think
wrongly if you
please,
but in all
cases
think for
yourself.

**DORIS
LESSING**

236

Nearly all men and women can stand
adversity, but if you want to test
a person's
character,
give them
power.

ANONYMOUS

237

You can't legislate good
will
that comes through
education.

**EL-HAJJ MALIK
EL-SHABAZZ**

238

Human beings, who are almost
unique
in having the
ability
to learn from the
experience
of others, are also
remarkable
for their apparent
disinclination
to do
so.

**DOUGLAS
ADAMS**

239

I think we are a
product
of all our
experiences.

**SANFORD I.
WEILL**

240

The hardest
struggle
of all is to be
something
different from
what
the average man
is.

**ROBERT H.
SCHULLER**

241

Nobody can give you
freedom.
Nobody can give you
equality
or justice or
anything.
If you're a
man,
you take
it.

**EL-HAJJ MALIK
EL-SHABAZZ**

242

There's a crack in
everything.
That's how the light gets
in.

**LEONARD
COHEN**

243

"But"
is a
fence
over which few
leap.

**GERMAN
PROVERB**

244

Chaos
is inherent in
all
compounded things.
Strive
on with
diligence.

BUDDHA

245

It's not patriotism when you say my country, right or wrong.

CINDY SHEEHAN

246

You're not supposed to be so
blind
with patriotism that you can't
face
reality. Wrong is
wrong,
no matter who says
it.

**EL-HAJJ MALIK
EL-SHABAZZ**

247

All
great achievements require
time.

MAYA
ANGELOU

248

If a policy is
wrongheaded,
feckless and
corrupt,
I take it personally and
consider
it a moral obligation to sound
off
and not shut
up
until it's
fixed.

**DAVID
HACKWORTH**

249

Believe nothing, no matter
where
you read it, or
who
said it, no matter if
I
have said it, unless it
agrees
with your
own
reason and
your
own common
sense.

BUDDHA

250

I'm fed
up
to the
ears
with old
men
dreaming up wars for
young
men to die
in.

**GEORGE
MCGOVERN**

251

War
is the unfolding of
miscalculations.

**BARBARA
TUCHMAN**

252

War would
end
if the dead could
return.

**STANLEY
BALDWIN**

253

You never suffer from a money problem, you always suffer from an idea problem.

ROBERT H. SCHULLER

254

Grab the broom of
anger
and drive
off
the beast of
fear.

**ZORA NEALE
HURSTON**

255

Can anything be
stupider
than that a man has the
right
to kill me because he
lives
on the other side of a
river
and his ruler has a
quarrel
with mine, though
I
have not quarreled with
him?

**BLAISE
PASCAL**

256

Mankind
must put an end to
war
before war puts an end to
mankind.

**JOHN F.
KENNEDY**

257

There is no greater
agony
than bearing an
untold
story inside
you.

**MAYA
ANGELOU**

258

Protectors of this
world
and guardians of the
ways
of Gods and Buddhas, the
techniques
of peace
enables
us to meet every
challenge.

259

I am an
ordinary
person who has been blessed with
extraordinary
opportunities and experiences.
Today
is one of those
experiences.

**SONIA
SOTOMAYOR**

260

It may be hard for an egg to turn
into a bird: it would be a jolly sight
harder for it to learn to fly while
remaining an egg. We are like eggs
at present. And you cannot go on
indefinitely being just an ordinary,
decent egg. We must be hatched
or go
bad.

**C.S.
LEWIS**

261

Life
is what
we
make
it.
Always has
been.
Always will
be.

**GRANDMA
MOSES**

262

Life
belongs to the
living,
and he who
lives
must be prepared for
changes.

**JOHANN WOLFGANG
VON GOETHE**

263

He who
rejects
change is the architect of
decay.
The only human
institution
which rejects
progress
is the
cemetery.

HAROLD WILSON

264

We must develop and maintain the capacity
to forgive. He who is
devoid
of the power to forgive is
devoid
of the power to love. There is
some
good in the worst of us and
some
evil in the best of us. When
we
discover this,
we
are less prone to hate our
enemies.

**MARTIN LUTHER
KING, JR.**

265

It takes but one
positive
thought when given a
chance
to survive and
thrive
to overpower an entire
army
of negative
thoughts.

**ROBERT H.
SCHULLER**

266

Do I contradict
myself?
Very well, then I contradict
myself,
I am
large,
I contain
multitudes.

**WALT
WHITMAN**

267

Don't rob yourself the
joy
of this
season
by wishing
you
were in a
future
or a past
one.

**CHERYL
BIEHL**

268

History,
despite its wrenching
pain,
cannot be
unlived,
but if
faced
with courage,
need
not be lived
again.

**MAYA
ANGELOU**

269

Wisdom
is knowing what to do next.
Skill
is knowing how to do it.
Virtue
is doing
it.

**DAVID STARR
JORDAN**

270

Never
wound a snake; kill
it.

**HARRIET
TUBMAN**

271

When one door
closes,
another one
opens,
but we often
look
so long and regretfully at the
closed
door that we fail to see the
one
that has opened for
us.

ALEXANDER GRAHAM BELL

272

Happiness is everyday
living
seen through a
veil.

**ZORA NEALE
HURSTON**

273

If we don't
change,
we don't
grow.
If we don't
grow,
we aren't really
living.

**GAIL
SHEEHY**

274

Battle
is the most magnificent
competition
in which a human being can
indulge.

**GEORGE S.
PATTON**

275

The world hates
change,
yet it is the only
thing
hat has brought
progress.

**CHARLES
KETTERING**

276

Time is the
coin
of your
life.
It is the only
coin
that you have, and only you can
determine
how it will be
spent.
Be careful
lest
you let other people
spend
it for
you.

**CARL
SANDBURG**

277

If you have no
critics
you'll likely have no
success.

**EL-HAJJ MALIK
EL-SHABAZZ**

278

The first
step
in the
acquisition
of wisdom is
silence,
the second
listening,
the third
memory,
the fourth
practice,
the fifth teaching
others.

**SOLOMON IBN
GABRIOL**

279

Love
is like a
virus.
It can happen to
anybody
at any
time.

MAYA ANGELOU

280

Do not
overrate
what you have
received,
nor envy others. He who
envies
others does not
obtain
peace of
mind.

BUDDHA

281

Always give a
word
or sign of
salute
when meeting or
passing
a friend, or even a
stranger,
if in a lonely
place.

TECUMSEH

282

An insincere and evil
friend
is more to be
feared
than a wild
beast;
a wild
beast
may wound your
body,
but an evil
friend
will wound your
mind.

BUDDHA

283

May God make
you
useful to
others.

**MUSLIM
PROVERB**

284

If we could sell our
experiences
for what they
cost
us, we'd all be
millionaires.

**ABIGAIL
VAN BUREN**

285

Wars
have never
hurt
anybody except the people who
die.

**SALVADOR
DALI**

286

Nothing is a
waste
of time if you
use
the experience
wisely.

**AUGUSTE
RODIN**

287

Just because
everything
is different doesn't
mean
anything has
changed.

288

If there is
anything
that we wish to
change
in the child, we should first
examine
it and see whether it is not
something
that could
better
be changed in
ourselves.

CARL
JUNG

289

The ache for home
lives
in all of us, the safe
place
where we can
go
as we
are
and not be
questioned.

MAYA ANGELOU

290

Never
cut a tree
down
in the wintertime.
Never
make a negative
decision
in the low time.
Never
make your most important
decisions
when you
are
in your worst
moods.

**ROBERT H.
SCHULLER**

291

Be grateful even for
hardship,
setbacks, and bad people.
Dealing
with such obstacles is an
essential
part of
training
in the Art of
Peace.

**MORIHEI
UESHIBA**

292

In a progressive
country
change is
constant;
change is
inevitable.

**BENJAMIN
DISRAELI**

293

We live in a moment of
history
where change is so
speeded
up that we begin to
see
the present only
when
it is already
disappearing.

**R. D.
LAING**

294

Without change, something
sleeps
inside us, and seldom
awakens.
The sleeper must
awaken.

**FRANK
HERBERT**

295

I'm for
truth,
no matter who tells it.
I'm for
justice,
no matter who it's for or
against.

**EL-HAJJ MALIK
EL-SHABAZZ**

296

True success is the
person
who invented
himself.

AL
GOLDSTEIN

297

If you're in a bad
situation,
don't worry it'll
change.
If you're in a good
situation,
don't worry it'll
change.

**JOHN A.
SIMONE, SR.**

298

Better than a
thousand
hollow words, is
one
word that brings
peace.

BUDDHA

299

Things alter for the worse
spontaneously,
if they be
not
altered for the better
designedly.

**FRANCIS
BACON**

300

I've learned that people
will
forget what you
said,
people will forget what you
did,
but people will never
forget
how you made them
feel.

**MAYA
ANGELOU**

301

Remember no one can
make
you feel
inferior
without your
consent.

**ELEANOR
ROOSEVELT**

302

All that we are is the
result
of what we have
thought.
If a man speaks or acts with an
evil
thought, pain follows him. If a
man
speaks or acts with a
pure
thought, happiness follows
him,
like a
shadow
that never leaves
him.

BUDDHA

303

Problems
are not stop
signs,
they are
guidelines.

ROBERT H.
SCHULLER

304

The riches in the
heart
can not be
stolen.

**RUSSIAN
PROVERB**

305

You must be the
change
you wish to
see
in the
world.

**MOHANDAS K.
GHANDI**

306

You can't
separate peace from
freedom
because no one can be at
peace
unless he has his
freedom.

**EL-HAJJ MALIK
EL-SHABAZZ**

307

Hatred does not cease by
hatred,
but only by
love;
this is the eternal
rule.

BUDDHA

308

Power
never takes a back
step
only in the
face
of more
power.

**EL-HAJJ MALIK
EL-SHABAZZ**

309

If we take the generally
accepted
definition of
bravery
as a quality which knows no
fear,
I have never seen a brave
man.
All men are
frightened.
The more
intelligent
they are, the
more
they are
frightened.

**GEORGE S.
PATTON**

310

Failure
is the
key
to success; Each
mistake
teaches us
something.

MORIHEI
UESHIBA

311

Perhaps travel cannot prevent
bigotry,
but by demonstrating that all
peoples
cry, laugh, eat, worry, and
die,
it can introduce the
idea
that if we try and
understand
each other,
we
may even become
friends.

**MAYA
ANGELOU**

312

Choose a job you
love,
and you will
never
have to work a
day
in your
life.

CONFUCIOUS

313

No.
Try not.
Do...
or do
not.
There is no
try.

YODA

314

When you are through
changing,
you are
through.

315

Look at a
day
when you are
supremely
satisfied at the end.
It
is not a
day
when you lounge around doing
nothing;
it is when you have had
everything
to do and
you
have done
it.

MARGARET THATCHER

316

The truth of the
matter
is that you always
know
the right thing to
do.
The hard
part
is doing
it.

**ROBERT H.
SCHULLER**

317

Any change, even a change
for the better, is always accompanied
by drawbacks and discomforts.

ARNOLD BENNETT

318

They must often
change,
who would be
constant
in happiness or
wisdom.

CONFUCIOUS

319

When your time comes to die,
be
not like those whose hearts are
filled
with fear of death, so that when
their
time comes they weep and pray
for
a little more time to live their
lives
over again in a different
way.
Sing your death song, and
die
like a hero going
home.

TECUMSEH

320

It's human
nature
to start
taking
things for
granted
again when
danger
isn't banging loudly on the
door.

**DAVID
HACKWORTH**

321

It is
foolish
and wrong to
mourn
the men who
died.
Rather we should thank
God
that such men
lived.

GEORGE S. PATTON

322

Prejudice
is a burden that
confuses
the past,
threatens
the future
and renders the present
inaccessible.

**MAYA
ANGELOU**

323

At the instant a
Warrior
confronts a
foe,
All things come into
focus.

**MORIHEI
UESHIBA**

324

I had
reasoned
this out in my
mind,
there was one of two
things
I had a right to,
liberty
or death;
if I could not have
one,
I would have the
other.

**HARRIET
TUBMAN**

325

Ambition
is like love,
impatient
both of delays and
rivals.

BUDDHA

326

You don't have to be a
man
to fight for
freedom.
All you have to
do
is to
be
an intelligent human
being.

**EL-HAJJ MALIK
EL-SHABAZZ**

327

Turn
your
scars
into
stars.

**ROBERT H.
SCHULLER**

328

Only the
dead
have seen the
end
of the
war.

**GEORGE
SANTAYANA**

329

Life
is but a moment,
death
also is but
another.

**ROBERT H.
SCHULLER**

330

War will exist until that
distant
day when the conscientious
objector
enjoys the same
reputation
and prestige that
the
warrior does
today.

**JOHN F.
KENNEDY**

331

We emphasize that we
believe
in change because we were
born
of it, we have
lived
by it, we prospered and grew
great
by it. So the status
quo
has never been our
god,
and we ask no one else to
bow
down before
it.

**CARL T.
ROWAN**

332

War is an ugly
thing,
but not the ugliest of
things.
The decayed and degraded
state
of moral and patriotic
feeling
which thinks that
nothing
is worth
war
is much
worse.

**JOHN STUART
MILL**

333

If you have only
one
smile in you
give
it to the people you
love.

**MAYA
ANGELOU**

334

Without accepting the fact that everything
changes, we cannot find perfect
composure. But unfortunately, although
it is true, it is difficult
for us to accept
it. Because we cannot
accept the truth
of transience, we suffer.

SHUNRYU SUZUKI

335

We all have big
changes
in our lives
that are more or less a second
chance.

**HARRISON
FORD**

336

Experience
is the
teacher
of all
things.

337

We allow our
ignorance
to prevail upon
us
and make
us
think we can survive
alone,
alone in patches,
alone
in groups, alone in
races,
even alone in
genders.

**MAYA
ANGELOU**

338

A single twig
breaks,
but the bundle of twigs is
strong.

TECUMSEH

339

Lord,
I'm going to hold
steady
on to
You
and You've
got
to see me
through.

**HARRIET
TUBMAN**

340

All wrong-doing
arises
because of
mind.
If mind is
transformed
can wrong-doing
remain?

BUDDHA

341

The only place where
your
dream becomes
impossible
is in your own
thinking.

**ROBERT H.
SCHULLER**

342

If everyone is
thinking
alike, then somebody isn't
thinking.

**GEORGE S.
PATTON**

343

If you
find
it in
your
heart to
care
for somebody
else,
you will have
succeeded.

**MAYA
ANGELOU**

344

I love
America
more than any other
country
in this world, and,
exactly
for this
reason,
I insist on the
right
to criticize her
perpetually.

**JAMES A.
BALDWIN**

345

And so, my fellow
Americans,
ask not what your
country
can do for you;
ask
what you can
do
for your
country?

**JOHN F.
KENNEDY**

346

Peace
begins with a
smile.

**MOTHER
THERESA**

347

A sense of
humor
is the ability to understand a
joke
and that the joke is
oneself.

CLIFTON PAUL FADIMAN

348

I have no
country
to fight for; my
country
is the
earth,
and I am a
citizen
of the
world.

**EUGENE V.
DEBS**

349

I think that people want
peace
so much that
one
of these days
government
had better get out of their
way
and let them have
it.

**DWIGHT D.
EISENHOWER**

350

Never
give up!
Never give up!
Never give
up!

**WINSTON
CHURCHILL**

351

Patriotism is
supporting
your country all the
time,
and your
government
when it deserves
it.

352

I
have long believed that
sacrifice
is the pinnacle of
patriotism.

353

I long, as does every human
being,
to be at
home
wherever I find
myself.

**MAYA
ANGELOU**

354

One of the definitions of
sanity
is the
ability
to tell
real
from unreal. Soon we'll
need
a new
definition.

**ALVIN
TOFFLER**

355

It is not easy to
see
how the more
extreme
forms of
nationalism
can long survive when
men
have seen the Earth in its true
perspective
as a single small
globe
against the
stars.

**ARTHUR C.
CLARKE**

356

Patriotism is not short, frenzied
outbursts of
emotion,
but the tranquil and steady
dedication
of a
lifetime.

ADLAI E.
STEVENSON

357

The direct use of
force
is such a poor
solution
to any
problem,
it is generally
employed
only by small
children
and large
nations.

**DAVID
FRIEDMAN**

358

If we don't end
war,
war will end
us.

H. G.
WELLS

359

The future
belongs
to those who
prepare
for it
today.

**EL-HAJJ MALIK
EL-SHABAZZ**

360

Anyone who thinks there's
safety
in numbers hasn't
looked
at the stock market
pages.

361

One may
know
how to gain a
victory,
and know not
how
to use
it.

**PEDRO CALDERON
DE LA BARCA**

362

Martyrs
are needed to create incidents.
Incidents
are needed to create revolutions.
Revolutions
are needed to create
progress.

**CHESTER
HIMES**

363

Toleration and
liberty
are the
foundations
of a great
republic.

**FRANK LLOYD
WRIGHT**

364

And your very
flesh
shall be a great
poem.

365

The
beginning
is always
today.

**MARY
WOLLSTONECRAFT**

366

When you rise in the
morning,
give thanks for the
light,
for your life, for your
strength.
Give thanks for your
food
and for the joy of
living.
If you
see
no reason to give
thanks,
the fault lies in
yourself.

TECUMSEH

DEEP APPRECIATION &
THANK YOU'S

THE CREATOR.
The Tolliver family: near, far and abroad:
Stephen/Sue, Courtney, McKenzie Tolliver,
Judy & Jesse Bey, Booper, Tank, Lafe/Judy, Darren,
Bradley, Rachel John , Sophia, Sylvia, Starr,
Merry Lavant, Lenard, Chanel, Lil' William, Josh,
Chris, Robin, Jaden, Brooklyn, Nathan Douglass, Dougie,
Natalie, Maurice, Danny, Sandy, Ray, Kylie, Meena,
Barbara & Sandy Summers, Kimson Albert, Abby Addis,
Laura Checkoway, Amy Linden, Candice Crossley, Paul,
Elysha and Gabriel Bixler, Jee Kim, Mrs. Harris,
Jake-ann Jones, Vinay Chowdhry, Andrienne,
Dakoit Pictures, GoboHD, Sharon Pendana,
JP Cummings, Zachary Ludescher, Stella Tan-Torres,
Sheril Antonio, Reggie/Akim Osse & family,
Raymond Todd, Nansi and Brandon Borum, Lee Borum,
Peter Stern & Family, Ruth Hochman,
Lisa Weldon, Michelle Auerbach, Supriya Pillai,
Jennifer Demme-Harris, Tamara/India Daley,
Crystal Whaley, Joan Van Hess, Gail Huggins Porter,
Natalie Jessica Ortiz, Hazel/Linden & family,
Robin Roberts and family, Miguel Deoliveira,
Walter Mudu, Fritz Celestine, Lauren Moore,
Drea Benedict, Debi & Josh Beckles, Denise Webb,
Mike & Nova Gallacchio, Ike Huff, Chris Corso,
Jamie Warner, Joan Van Hees, Sandy Wilson,
Beth Perotti, Priscilla Perotti-Igram, Sherwyn Smith,
Garland Farwell, Jake Utsey, Fiona Bloom,
Kate Daniels-Kurtz, Ali Daniels, Doug Carter,
Assaf Ziv, Brian Cohen, Dominique Brown, Vipal Monga,
Nick Charles, Michael, Beatriz & Manuel Smith,
Emir & Denise Lewis, Ayo, Cosi, Khari Lewis, Dave
Ratzlow, Sherwyn Smith, Abdul & Cassandra, Sonia,
Abistro Restaurant, Mike Thompson/Brooklyn Moon,

DEEP APPRECIATION & THANK YOU'S

The Hill Staff: Howard, DK, Michelle Herrera,
Fort Greene, BKNY, Anne Kristof, Marlon Styles,
Marcel Bassett, Mia Parker, Jud Laghi, Molly Secours,
Kathy Conkwright, Stephanie Johnson,
The Kiwi Space Girl Jackie Maw, Sarah Gonzales-Myers,
Joy and Justin Green, Susan and Jack Daniels,
Mary Lou Petro, Richard Milter, Toni Dubois,
Gina Paige. KAF Deli, All Seasons/ECHOS, KAF,
Betsy Whelan, Kervin Simms,
22nd MPAD/Kandahar, Afghanistan: MAJ Desantis,
1SG Herron, SFC Couture, SFC Coble, SGT Rosencranz,
SSG Rader, CPL Gloria Sala, SSG Anishka Calder,
SGT Green, SGT Pike, PFC Rollins, SPC Collier,
PFC Baldon, SSG Calder, SPC Erickson, TSGT Heiser,
CPT Villarreal, CPT Tobias, SSGT Jones, SSGT Mills,
SSGT Flaherty, CPT Scott, CPT Gothard, CPT Weece,
SGT Graff, MC1 Sherman, PO2 Garza, PO3 Burnside,
SGT Florence, SPC Hauk, SPC Booth, SrA Ingalsbe,
SrA Bell. TEAM CANADA: Corey, Nate, Hughes, Millar,
Casey, Tom, Jerry, Jay, CPT Brooks, Wallace.
USFOR-A SOUTH: MSG Munez-Dones,
MSG William Malachi III. BRAGG: SSG Dane Calder,
SGT Herff, TSGT Hasennauer, Col. Walter E. Kurtz,
LTC William "Bill" Kilgore, CPT Benjamin L. Willard,
PO3 Jay "Chef" Hicks, PO3 Lance B. Johnson,
PO3 Tyrone "Mr. Clean" Miller, QM George Phillips,
SGT David Mclean, SPC DeArmas.

If I forgot you—my bad. Print your name here:

_____

and last but not least:
J. BIRD LATHON bka THE BIRD OF PREY
Mad Genius/Alchemist/Creative Conspirator/Designer.
Thank you for helping make this book possible.

BIO

Gabriel Tolliver is currently serving in the US Army as a broadcast journalist. He is known as a "creative mothership" across media platforms of film/TV/new media and publishing.

Prior to joining the Army to seek out new stories to tell and pay down his bills, he was a Brooklyn based freelance writer/producer/director. He has created content for such notable entities such as MTV, VH1, Current TV, Sesame Street and for numerous independent productions.

He is also the co-author of BLING: The Hip-Hop Jewelry Book-the definitive book on Hip-Hip culture's love affair with jewelry.

Gabriel makes his home where ever his feet touch the ground. You can contact him at: creativemothership@gmail.com

"

DEPLOYMENT
BY DESIGN
THE MAKING OF

EMBRACE
THE SUCK
366 DAYS OF
STRENGTH,
COURAGE,
INSPIRATION,
WISDOM
AND HOPE

BY GABRIEL A. TOLLIVER

DEPLOYMENT BY DESIGN
The making of EMBRACE THE SUCK
DESIGNER'S INTRODUCTION

This is a print version of the blog sharing the process of creating the new book of inspirational quotes written by the co - author of *Bling! The Hip Hop Jewelry Book.*

This was written in response to questions about my process - and the collective process with the author - and to reveal the intended meanings within the final product that are not visible on the page.

I am also sharing the conceptual sketches and designs for *Embrace the Suck* as well to illustrate how important drawing is to my approach to a project. The lines, which may seem like meaningless scribbles to some, are very important mental musings on the method to make the messages meaningful.

I have applied the same design principles to this section as executed in the book, to keep as sense of consistency for the whole publication.

When Gabe decided to include my articulation of the aesthetics of this book again I was flattered by the fact he felt it important enough to include with the important words from these important figures he's selected for this first volume.

I hope you have enjoyed reading *Embrace the Suck* as much as I have enjoyed designing it.

J Bird Lathon
Artist + Designer + Filmmaker

DEPLOYMENT BY DESIGN
The making of EMBRACE THE SUCK

The question was seemingly simple. How could the apprehension and adrenaline rush felt while training for combat deployment, be visually represented in a book written to process that rush of complex emotions and actions?

The question was posed by Gabriel Tolliver, who after almost twenty years as a filmmaker, multimedia artist and writer, enlisted in the US Army in 2007 at the age of 41 to discover new stories and experiences to tell.

Tolliver had co-authored the book *Bling: The Hip-Hop Jewelry Book* which was published in 2006 by Bloomsbury Press. The book became a definitive pop culture book on urban style and yielded a popular YouTube video called "How To Make Fresh Diamonds In The Microwave". The clip and its claim were also explored on an episode of the television show *Mythbusters* in April of 2009.

Once Tolliver was thoroughly engaged in his enlistment and boot camp training, he would return to writing again, but for extremely different reasons than before. Tolliver needed to process his 'buildup of anxiety, stress and fear' before his deployment to Afghanistan for Operation Enduring Freedom as a "46 Romeo" (Army Broadcast Journalist) in 2009. Finding strength in quotes from some of his favorite historical figures and writers, he compiled *Embrace the Suck: 366 Days of Strength, Courage, Inspiration and Hope.* This collection of inspirational quotations was intended for his battle buddies and their families, with hope the words would 'connect to something inside you' and make the first year of deployment transpire with less difficulty.

Gabriel had already taken the long flight on a C-130 cargo plane to Kandahar Airfield (KAF) in Afghanistan and was mentally in combat mode when I received the first manuscript in November of 2009. I quickly reviewed the quotes, dedications and his introduction. It was typical Gabe. The quotes were diverse as they were descriptive and pointed as they were poignant. I was just stoked to be asked to one of the first to read it.

In telephone calls and emails, sometimes interrupted by insurgent mortar attacks and unscheduled sorties, Gabriel articulated his thoughts on the design of the book. Tolliver wanted the

DEPLOYMENT BY DESIGN
The making of EMBRACE THE SUCK

apprehension and adrenaline rush within the complex emotions of combat deployment to be visually represented on the page. He also desired a no-nonsense, 'government issue' design sensibility to reflect the machinations of the US Army itself. With the emotional content and aesthetic intent defined Gabe requested I have a 'go at it', reinforcing the need for an irreverent approach to designing inspirational compendiums.

Accepting the challenge, I ruminated on the content and started to consider it aesthetically. I wanted to achieve a way to incisively allow the quotes to speak visually without overshadowing them emotionally. Work on the design did not start right away as I was engaged in pitching and promoting my documentary and creating an animatic for an animated short simultaneously, but the weight of the words stayed with me as I worked on these other projects. I wanted to get this right as I could appreciate Gabe's intent with the book.

I grew up in Clarksville, Tennessee which borders on Fort Campbell, Kentucky, one of the largest Army bases in the country. Growing up in an 'Army town' populated by so many members of the 'Screaming Eagles' of the 101st Airborne allowed me a unique perspective on how deployment affects soldiers and their families.

My experience with the changes in personality and sense of purpose our friends, brothers, mothers, fathers, sons and daughters possess once they have returned home was being primed to manifest itself in other military themed projects.

When Gabe presented me with this one he wanted to draw upon that untapped energy and intent for *Embrace The Suck*. He also stated he dug the design sensibility of our previous media collaborations that were put on hold due to his deployment, and wanted to continue in that vein.

Once I had some down time between tasks on the film projects I began working on the visual approach to *Embrace the Suck* by sketching on paper and working in Photoshop, exploring layouts and manipulating type and images.

Nothing to my liking came from these early attempts except crumpled paper balls used as last second game winning shots in imaginary basketball games or digital files destined for the recycle bin.

DEPLOYMENT BY DESIGN
The making of EMBRACE THE SUCK

The first real breakthrough happened while dreaming in the early morning on the fourth of March in 2010. In a multilayered haze of images and text that would momentarily perplex the movie mind of Harold Crick, there it was. The words and punctuation marks were moving toward the margins as if pulled by magnets. When the movement was complete the two meanings of the word deploy were arranged on facing pages with examples of their usage as if from a dictionary.

There was the answer to the question, brought to me again by another session of lucid dreaming.

I got out of bed and made the first sketch. I laid out the facing pages first and then a small thumbnail of the cover. I determined the height of the letters and the inner and outer margins based on the Createspace specs Gabe had forwarded to me. Just from the sketch alone I thought there would be some interesting linear beauty to the quotes if arranged this way.

About a week later I emailed Gabe about the book and my idea about it. I told him I wanted to apply the meanings of the word deploy - to act as organizing principles for the design of the book. He dug it from the verbal description alone and gave me the go ahead to create some preliminaries when time permitted.

I had to return to work on my doc *Black Moses and the Golden Idol*, and short film *The Ride* before attending the Nashville Film Festival. I didn't make any new sketches until the twentieth of April.

The first was an image of the cover. This is the initial instance when I could see how the iconography could be carried out from cover to cover. The second sketch was a layout on quarter inch grid paper, finalizing sizes of quote numbers, attributions and margins.

Two days later I started working on the execution of the book in earnest. I reacquainted myself with the meanings of deploy again in the dictionary. I sometimes like to create a visual image of the meaning of a word (as it is on the page) to use it as a point of departure to reinforce or refute the meaning.

I felt the final result would be referential to authorship, warfare and diplomacy through the use of typography, geometry and iconography.

DEPLOYMENT BY DESIGN
The making of EMBRACE THE SUCK

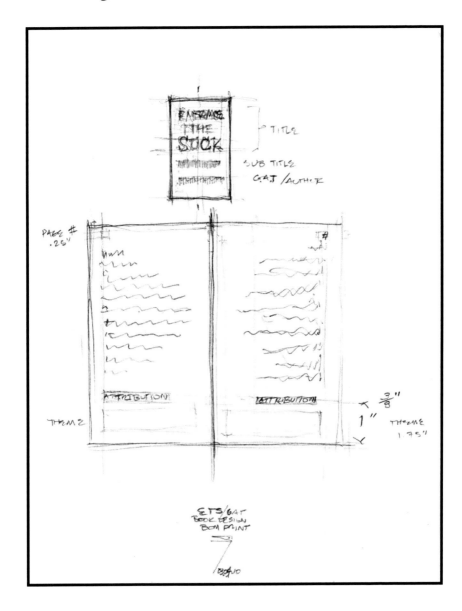

The first sketch for the single and double page spreads for *Embrace the Suck* created on March 04, 2010. The thumbnail of the cover would change in later designs, with the title being adjusted to only being two lines instead of three to make room for the subtitle.

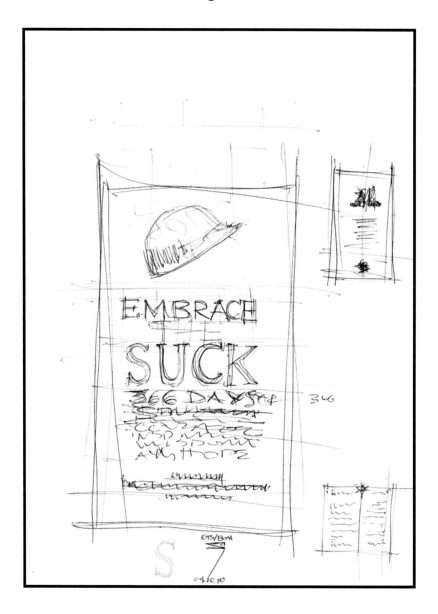

The second sketch for single and double page spreads created on April 20, 2010. Here the subtitle and iconography are being worked out in relation to the main title and proportion of the book. This is also the first appearance of the empty boots.

DEPLOYMENT BY DESIGN
The making of **EMBRACE THE SUCK**

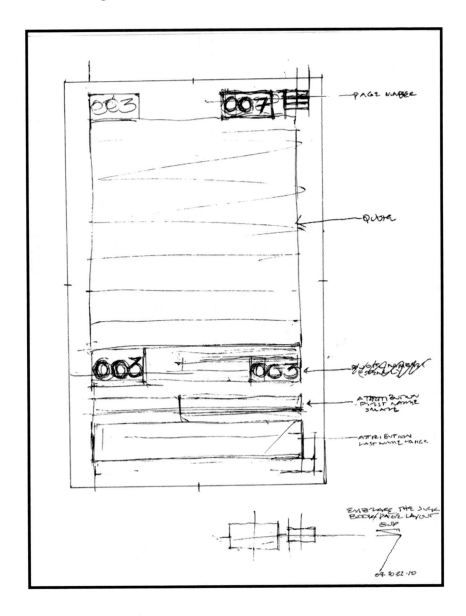

This drawing on grid paper created on April 20 - 22, 2010 defines the actual height of page numbers, quote numbers, attributions and space was needed to accommodate more lengthy quotations. A horizontal orientation was considered as seen the bottom, right of center.

DEPLOYMENT BY DESIGN
The making of EMBRACE THE SUCK

I created a template and started working, ready to copy, paste and
print this book to life.

The first task was the defining the type. Quotations are numbered
using stenciled digits typically used by the US Army. The
quotations themselves are rendered in a grungy typewriter style,
making reference to authorship and to Gabe himself.

Attributions were initially going to be represented in Helvetica Bold
but were changed to Eurostile, for its connotations with Cold War era
signage and title designs of utopian and dystopian feature films. The
peaceful nature of some of these luminaries quoted, adds a bit of
irony to the use of these types as well.

Next, the deliberate justification of the copy on the page was tested
using the longest quote in the book. I treated the outer margins like
geographic borders, arranging words so they seem ready to 'deploy'
off the page. A two page spread reveals a large amount of white
space between quotes, making reference to the large amount of
down time between missions or attacks. This also gives the reader
the space to make personal notes or reflections, letting their own
words coexist with ones on the printed page. Gabriel made it a point
to insure that.

The specific sentence arrangement is for descriptive emphasis.
I applied one rule when executing this: every other line should be a
word of importance in the sentence. When odd and even lines are
read separately after doing this, nouns and modifiers create quotes
within the quote. At times the actual length of words and sentences,
create visual haikus of size, shape and proportion on the page or
create some sense of destination before the punctuation does.

The justification and rules of arrangement for *Embrace the Suck* are
sometimes broken, but so are treaties. This is an allusion to the
illusion of war and how the futility of words can lead to it, but can
hopefully also lead us from it.

Finally, the iconography literally represents conveyances and tools of
and for deployment. The stark black on white images represents the
departure, combat awareness and eventual combat fatigue a soldier
will experience, exude and endure during their tour of duty.

QUOTATION NUMBERS

1234567890

STENCIL

(@ 44 PT)

"Quotations"

abcdefghijklmnopqrstuvwxyz

ABCDEFGHIJKLMNOPQRSTUVWXYZ

"..." ! , ? -

TYPEWRITER OLDSTYLE

(@ 20 pt)

ATTRIBUTIONS

ABCDEFGHIJKLMNOPQR STUVWXYZ -

EUROSTILE BOLD

(@ 27 PT)

Here the typography used for *Embrace The Suck* is juxtaposed to illustrate the contrast in clarity and construction. The practical, grungy and machined looking typography appealed to Gabriel and I as military history buffs (one now a veteran), graphic artists and filmmakers. During the design of this book we rediscovered our mutual affection for stenciled typography, official or otherwise, and have been creating original versions to incorporate in future Birds of Mothership projects.

213

192

I believe we are still so
innocent.
The species are still so
innocent
that a person who is apt to be
murdered
believes that the
murderer,
just before he puts the
final
wrench on his
throat,
will have enough
compassion
to give him one sweet cup of
water.

MAYA ANGELOU

191

212   213

192

The
beginning
is always
today.

I believe we are still so
innocent.
The species are still so
innocent
that a person who is apt to be
murdered
believes that the
murderer,
just before he puts the
final
wrench on his
throat,
will have enough
compassion
to give him one sweet cup of
water.

MARY WOLLSTONECRAFT

MAYA ANGELOU

Preliminary single and double page spreads created on April 22, 2010. Note the actual page numbers and quote numbers used together in this version with the attributions temporarily styled in Arial for reference.

DEPLOYMENT BY DESIGN
The making of EMBRACE THE SUCK

An Army helmet seen on the cover was the graphic point of departure for the icons. This was decided upon after several conversations with Gabe about our mutual love of some of the characterizations in the film *Full Metal Jacket* and his momentary appropriation of the name 'Private Joker' for motivation through boot camp. For me it also symbolized introspection and the mental states of a soldier in combat mode. I had heard several stories from veterans growing up and now can see the influence it had on me as a storyteller and this was a small way of acknowledging them.

The use of the C-130 Hercules cargo planes with punctuation came spontaneously while laying out the dedications page. I wanted to visually represent the actual commencement of the physical deployment by soldiers through that long, grueling flight to their station. When Gabe reviewed an early copy of the book, he really got the meaning of the use, and suggested we place another image of the aircraft 'returning home' near the end of the book.

The aviation images and punctuation used iconically, appears before what we felt was the most important image of the book. Very early on Gabe expressed the well worn and empty pair of boots be used to signify combat fatigue and the tour of duty coming to and end. To the enlisted on the front lines, this image is the ultimate gesture in honoring the loss of battle buddies in combat. This image is becoming more prevalent in the consciousness of civilians through its use stateside to bring attention to the casualties not always reported on the front pages. The traveling exhibition "Eyes Wide Open" is a great example of this.

Originally I had scaled my drawing of the boots on the back cover to be the same size as the helmet on the front cover. After Gabe reviewed the second version of the cover he decided he wanted to enlarge the image on the back and within as well, to emphasize the importance of the losses and its omnipresent possibility.

The drawing of the pair of empty boots was done in pen and ink then scanned and cleaned up in Photoshop for the final design. I wanted the boots to be appear rough or appear to be quickly drawn by a soldier on the frontlines or resemble an amateur tattoo. The final result is a balance of rough composition and emblematic execution, matching the additional icons used throughout.

The initial drawing for the pair of empty boots was partially completed with the intention to fully execute in Photoshop or Illustrator.

DEPLOYMENT BY DESIGN
The making of EMBRACE THE SUCK

The cover of the book went through a number of iterations before we settled on the bichromatic design we have now. The first design I submitted used a version of camouflage as the background, blurred to symbolize the intense heat of the intended destination in the desert. Gabe informed me that specific pattern of camouflage has been phased out in favour of a new, more effective one. He also stated that the use could be predictable and limiting.

The covers also featured the skull and crossbones version of the Creative Mothership logo that had been in use for Gabe's projects at that point. I had recently designed a logo for Birds Of Mothership, the newly minted rebranding for Gabe's media company.
He decided Embrace the Suck would be the first project to bear the new name so we incorporated the otherworldly image into the design as well.

So with these notes and directions I went back to the digital drawing board and started looking for new colors and layouts to go with. It led me back to the desert again and I suggested a tan colour to make reference to the sand found in Kandahar. We both felt that colour was not going to come off as well as we expected in the print process with Createspace.

I tried another, a nice shade of terra cotta. This color just spoke to me and upon thinking about the choice it made sense. While in boot camp and journalism school, Gabe used to take R&R in Arizona, the current home of his mother and other relatives. This color is very present in the landscape and structure of the state. I first fell in love with this color and material as an Architecture student, discovering the Southwestern work (specifically in Arizona) of Frank Lloyd Wright.

With the cover design complete and to our liking, I executed the remainder of the book with InDesign. As Gabe would tweak the contents of the book, I would refine the design of each quote and send PDFs via email to him to review.

Our editing process consisted of deleting and adding quotes, editing the sequence and number of quotes by attributors to accentuate themes or to prevent monotony and repetition. I created an Excel spreadsheet (and template for subsequent editions of ETS) for Gabe to filter and review the quotes or to make additions to

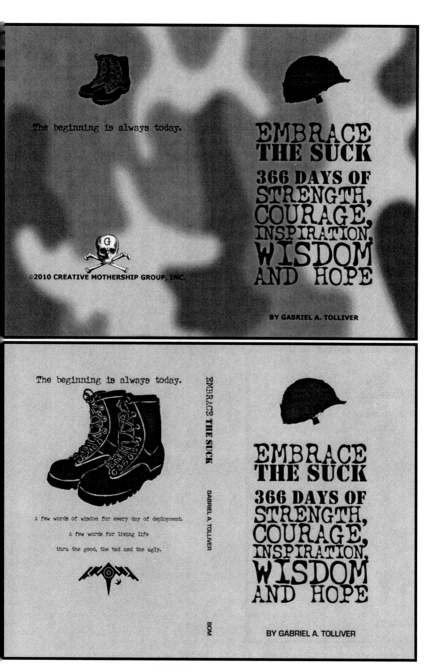

Preliminary covers created on April 22 and May 31, 2010.

DEPLOYMENT BY DESIGN
The making of EMBRACE THE SUCK

The final cover design was created on June 6, 2010. The final page layout shows the deliberate non use of page numbers. Gabe wanted the quote numbers serve as a calendar, as the days spent on the front lines is the most important number to many.

DEPLOYMENT BY DESIGN
The making of EMBRACE THE SUCK

This series of avatars and icons were designed spontaneously in the early morning of September 21, for Gabe's personal use on *Embrace the Suck* profiles online. These are variations of the iconography that will be utilized for the official website. The first design without the titles features quotation marks as used in the book and abstractly resemble the way cartridges for machine guns are strapped to helmets. This was another way of referencing the film *Full Metal Jacket* as the poster design made this habit famous.

DEPLOYMENT BY DESIGN
The making of EMBRACE THE SUCK

When viewed in this sequence, the icons illustrate the story of Gabe's journey though his tour of duty, from basic training to his return.

submit to me for inclusion. The spreadsheet allowed me a method of documenting the changes with an easy way to copy and paste those changes into InDesign.

Gabe let me get in on the act and I submitted two quotations, numbers 362 and 363. I will let you discover who they are and what they said by reading the book. Those who know my work and influences will not be surprised by their identities.

We settled upon a final copy on June 1ST and submitted it to Createspace to order our first proofs. Over the next few weeks we dealt with upload issues with Createspace and tweaked the design and contents a bit more. I received my first copy on July 22ND, and felt our intentions with the content and designs were successful. As a designer or any creative person that engages in an expressive endeavour, it's intimate moments with the final product that are the most important and fulfilling. No amount of accolades can ever replace that.

Gabe made it back to the states safely. He is currently fulfilling the last few days of his obligations with the 22nd Mobile Public Affairs Detachment based out of Fort Bragg, NC. Upon his full discharge we will begin to promote the book even more and execute the multimedia aspects of *Embrace The Suck* that will appear on the internet and mobile devices.

I hope you enjoy reading this book as much as I enjoyed designing it.

J Bird Lathon
Artist + Designer + Filmmaker
September 30, 2010

CPSIA information can be obtained at www.ICGtesting.com
Printed in the USA
LVOW072144051011

249324LV00006B/42/P